JACEK SARYUSZ-WOLSKI

Vice-President of the European People's Party

"Achieving success as an MEP, both nationally and within the EU, requires many skills - mastering the nuances of the legislative process, negotiating with impact, building networks, maximizing support and votes, organizing day-to-day functioning with optimal results, and many more. Marilyn Political's insightful tutorial captures these nuances in one book that every aspiring MEP and his collaborators should read."

ALEXANDER GRAF LAMBSDORFF

Vice-President of the European Parliament

"Unique and impressive. An absolute must-read for all new Members of the European Parliament."

PETRI SARVAMAA

Vice-Chair of the European Parliament's Committee on Budgets

"Astonishing read! It's merciless, unforgiving, and so true. As an MEP I could not imagine a better guide into ways of influencing political decision-making in Brussels. I regularly go back to the advice of the book. And I make sure all my advisers and assistants know the text by heart."

MARKUS FERBER

Vice-Chair of the European Parliament's Committee on Economic and Monetary Affairs

"How to Run the European Parliament provides an informed insight on what happens behind the curtains. From negotiation strategies to shaping public perceptions - this book is the perfect read if you want to gain an in-depth understanding of how European policy making actually works."

ANDREY NOVAKOV

Member of the European Parliament

"One of the most get-to-the-point, useful, and must-have political books I have in my library."

JONÁS FERNÁNDEZ

Member of the European Parliament

"This book makes for fascinating - and funny - reading. More importantly, it is quite useful, particularly for newcomers. I highly recommend it to any new MEP as absolutely essential. It provides quite a number of practical suggestions, and not to be underestimated, a fair amount of laughing, something that should never be in short supply when working at the European Parliament."

LINNÉA ENGSTRÖM

Vice-Chair of the European Parliament's
Committee on Fisheries

"This book will teach you the mind-set and psychology of the European Parliament. Being a European politician means: relying on good advisers and having the confidence and strength to be patient, generous, and trustworthy. The road to success lies in hard work - and making the right choices. This book will give you exactly the push you need, and the direction to set you on the right path."

SANDER LOONES

Vice-Chair of the European Parliament's
Committee on Economic and Monetary Affairs

"The European House of Cards, but with a healthy portion of pragmatism."

IVAN ŠTEFANEC

Member of the European Parliament

"The book is a very useful and enjoyable reading, particularly for newcomers to the European Parliament. It is a good overview of parliamentarian activities. It reassured me about what I was doing right and where I should improve."

HOW TO RUN THE EUROPEAN PARLIAMENT

MARILYN POLITICAL

CreateSpace Independent Publishing Platform
4900 Lacross Rd, North Charleston, SC 29406, USA

2nd edition
Copyright © 2015
MARILYN POLITICAL
Marton Kovacs, Koelblgasse 1/18, 1030 Vienna, Austria
All rights reserved.

1st edition published 2014

www.marilynpolitical.com
contact@marilynpolitical.com

ISBN-13: 978-1502542717
ISBN-10: 1502542714

CONTENTS

PROLOGUE

Welcome to the European Parliament. You made it. You have proven that you have the skills, the looks, and the charisma to get here. Now get ready to swim with the sharks. This book will teach you how.

You will learn how to become powerful, respected, and famous. You will know how to steer the legislative process and how to eliminate your competition. You will understand how to secure your reelection and how to dominate your national media landscape.

Do not expect any idealism. This book is about ruthless pragmatism. It is not about how the Parliament works. It is about making the Parliament work as you want it to work. Now let the games begin.

1

GAIN POWER

Whether you entered politics because you wanted to contribute to change or just to gain authority, you will always need power to achieve your goals. It will never be enough to have the best ideas and the finest arguments. You compete with 750 democratically elected Members of the European Parliament (MEPs), whose egos are just as big as yours. You will throughout your political career have to exert influence and overcome resistance in order to get what you want.

Keep in mind, therefore, the five rules of political power:

1. Political power requires support and respect.
2. The more support you have, the more influence you will hold.
3. The more respected you are, the less re-

sistance you will face.

4. Gain support by hiring, charming, and benefitting others.

5. Gain respect by demonstrating strength, competence, and importance.

Build your team, your network, and your reputation according to these postulates. Never rely on selfless solidarity or genuine gratitude. Play your strengths, and do not trust anyone.

1.1

BUILD YOUR TEAM

The first key to gaining power is to surround yourself with people who are more talented, experienced, and competent than you. Get them to work for you, and take the credit for everything they do.

Many Members of the European Parliament like to hire young graduates who are at the beginning of their careers. These young professionals are eager to follow and less likely to complain about unpleasant tasks or low salaries. They usually leave the European Parliament (EP), however, after one or two years in order to move on to their next career goals. Around two-thirds of all accredited parliamentary assistants stay shorter than the full term. As a consequence many MEPs lose their employees just when they were about to understand how to play the political game professionally. This high fluctuation and brain drain severely weaken the EP in the power struggle with the Commission and the Council and regularly lead to MEPs being defeated during trilogues by more experienced public servants.

Do not make these same mistakes. Only an amateur learns by experience. Dominate by profiting from others' experience. No matter how many terms you have already served in the EP, dare to hire people who are more clever and experienced than you. Always remember: experience equals power. Almost all successful MEPs who have made it into the EP's bureau have had assistants who served several legislative terms in the Parliament. The more experience your advisers have, the more you will dominate the EP.

You have a healthy monthly budget to spend on employees and political service providers. Invest the money in the most productive political minds and the best strategic thinkers. Look for reliable, proactive, and creative people instead of obedient executers and loyal party members. Break with political habits and choose candidates based solely on their skills and their added value for your political career. Make sure that they have political instinct and strong opinions, and that they share your values while daring to criticise your ideas. They must want to take responsibility, work well under pressure, and have strong interpersonal skills. In addition, they should have well-established networks and know all the procedural and political manoeuvres necessary to get things done.

There are plenty of politically sensitive issues in which you cannot or should not get involved personally. Your assistants' duty is to get the dirty work done for you and to take the heat off you. They have to be perceived as persistent, tough, and ruthless, while you remain liked and respected. Successful assistants are not popular. The ones who are liked by everyone have not fought hard enough.

Assume your leadership responsibilities, and determine everybody's role according to the priorities of your political work. Do not dominate your team. Dominate *with* your team. Wanting to do everything by yourself is a sign of weakness. Be the leader, have an overview, but delegate as much as possible. Avoid any hierarchies among your employees. Instead, define clear responsibilities and separate roles for each staff member, as follows:

Policy Adviser

In order to successfully influence the legislative process, you need a policy adviser in Brussels to follow the relevant parliamentary committees. Choose someone with contacts to the EP admin-istration and close ties to the Commission and the permanent representations of the Member States. Hire a creative and strategic thinker who grasps political opportunities immediately and knows how to translate them into legal amendments. He or she should understand how to cooperate with external stakeholders to obtain any necessary in-formation. Moreover, this expert has to be some-one with strong negotiation skills who can accom-plish the necessary majorities to get your proposals adopted.

Party Networker

In addition to your policy expert, you need a sym-pathetic local assistant to take care of your party and constituency duties. Never forget: you get nominated and elected at home. Hire, therefore, someone reliable, with strong interpersonal skills, who will represent you loyally. Focus on finding a talented organiser who can prepare any event and manage your political campaigns. He or she should be able to charm troubled constituents and not only maintain but also build your base locally. This person needs to be involved in all domestic issues and keep you constantly updated on the developments within your constituency. Most importantly, your party networker should have strong ties to your party's leadership, attend all relevant party events, and be sensitive to the general mood within your party.

Public Relations Manager

In addition to your policy and party experts, hire an experienced PR manager to influence the public opinion and shield you from intrusive reporters. Choose someone who is able to transform legal proposals into easily understandable political messages and to spin difficult topics successfully in your domestic media. This person should have excellent writing skills, an outstanding understanding of online tools, and most importantly a wide network of contacts among reporters on the European, national, and local level. The PR manager needs to draft your speeches, make sure your press releases get picked up, place your op-eds in the relevant newspapers, and organise your TV appearances. Avoid trusting your party's press people. They will always sacrifice you if it helps them avoid negative press for the party's leadership.

Personal Assistant

In addition to the three above-mentioned experts, make sure to hire a secretary in Brussels to run your day-to-day life. Hire someone with strong organisational skills and experience with the EP's administration. Your personal assistant should have a service attitude, host your guests, make coffee, book flights and hotels, run your errands, organise your events, keep track of your budget, and schedule your meetings. Respect everybody's role, and never ask any other employee to fulfil these tasks.

External Consultants

You are entitled to spend 25 per cent of your monthly budget on external service providers. Use this possibility to broaden your workforce by hiring independent political consultants. They have repeatedly proven to be key for exceling political careers and staying ahead of competition. Professional political consulting companies have a wider set of skills, a broader overview of political developments, and a larger network of relevant contacts than your employees do. In addition they have a less biased perspective and a more honest approach in highlighting for you the areas where further improvements may be necessary. Hire them to routinely support you in strategically defining your political brand, setting your political agenda, and streamlining your organisational set-up.

Make sure you stay away from external consultants who also receive funding from private companies or lobby associations. Even if they separate their duties fairly, the sheer fact that your consultants receive money from a certain special-interest group could already question your initiatives as biased and consequently unnecessarily endanger your political career.

Interns

When it comes to interns, forget everything mentioned above. Do not focus on an applicant's skills; focus only on your political profit. Do not hire someone random who applied by e-mail. Instead organise in cooperation with your local party a public competition for the best European intern. The aim is not to advertise the job; the aim is to advertise your close relationship with the party and the constituency. Try to gain from everything you do. Consequently do not hire the most talented constituent. Hire the one with the most influential parents in the party.

Once you have built a strong team, never stand still. Lead, coordinate, and motivate your employees continuously in order to form a united and dedicated workforce. Organise weekly meetings to plan upcoming events and analyse past achievements. Reflect regularly on your team's input and the achieved output. Dare to scrap activities that do not justify the effort. Always improve. Always analyse what you could do better.

Evaluate your team's work, and adapt and reorganise if necessary. Do not misinterpret political loyalty as a need to drag untalented employees along. Promote achievers, and dismiss underachievers. The stronger your team, the stronger you will be. It is your personal army. Buy their loyalty through high salaries and long vacations, and get them into influential positions after they leave you. Not only will they be your thankful servants, but also you will be able to exploit their new jobs' networks for your own benefit.

1.2
BUILD YOUR NETWORK

The second key to gaining power is to get the support of influential stakeholders. Charm them in order to benefit from their authority.

Understand the rules of the political game on the European level and get a sense where the power lays. Recognise which players are influential, and focus on getting close to them. Do not underestimate anybody's importance. Every single relationship and every personal favour can be useful one day. The bigger your political network, the more power you will have. Building your networks is therefore not about short-term gains but long-term alliances.

Win your national delegation over first, then move on to your political group's fellow committee members. They are the ones you will work with most. Focus next on establishing good relationships with the most influential people in your group, in particular your group's leader, bureau members, and coordinators. Then widen your network by targeting fellow committee colleagues from the other groups. You will not have any impact on the legislative process without their cooperation. Proceed step-by-step, until everybody knows and respects you. Study existing networks and interdependences, and detect possible allies and rivals. Whose standing may be helpful for you? Whose contacts can you benefit from? Whose influence can get you further? Identify the MEPs you can profit from most, and try to get their support.

While building your support base among fellow MEPs, do not forget the people running the machinery in the background. Try to establish friendly ties with the secretary-general of the EP and the secretaries-general of the political groups. They are usually involved in all important political decisions behind the scenes. In addition make sure to build close relationships with the public servants who are responsible for distributing allowances or can provide valuable contacts and information. Focus your attention especially on your committees' and political group's policy advisers. Their support is crucial for your legislative work's success.

Concentrate at the same time on the other European institutions. Build your contacts among the Commissioners and their cabinets as well as the Commission's legal service and relevant Directorates-General (DGs) in order to profit from their influence and expertise. Establish good relations with the Council's secretariat and the permanent representations of the Member States. Focus in particular on your Member State's diplomats and those of the upcoming presidencies, as well as the German and French diplomats. Without their support you will lack the power to significantly influence European policies. Cooperate closely to gain their trust.

While building your new networks, make sure not to neglect your home base. The importance of your constituency has not diminished just because you have moved to the European level. Continue to network on the domestic political level, and stay in close touch with your party's leadership (see also section 2.1).

At the same time, strategically build your network with domestic media representatives on the local, national, and European level. Furthermore, in order to increase your name recognition, try to establish contacts with respected authors, successful actors, and well-known artists. Good relations with the media are key for building your reputation and influencing public opinion (see also sections 4.1 and 4.2).

In addition to your political and media contacts, establish close ties to special-interest groups, in particular the ones supporting your party at home. Their support during political campaigns can often be very helpful. Do not forget: exclusive information is every lobbyist's currency. Offer lobbyists, therefore, special insights in exchange for needed background material or influential contacts. Work together proactively, and find out what other MEPs have told them about you and your initiatives. What is more, use supportive lobbyists for planting rumours and leaking information on undesired political developments.

Continuously expand your database of contacts, and reach out to everyone whose support might advance your career. Do not wait until you are approached. Use chance encounters by attending conferences, going to parliamentary meetings, and from time to time stopping by at Place du Luxembourg. Do not count on anybody's goodwill. Obtain the support you need by gaining sympathy and exchanging favours.

Gain Sympathy

Never neglect the social dimension. People who like you are more likely to support you. Always remember this simple fact of human behaviour. Personal apathy and sympathy often prevail over political lines or interests. Focus, therefore, on coming across as friendly, approachable, and authentic.

Try to remember the names and faces of everyone you meet. Adapt to each person's social and cultural background. Stress the topics they want to talk about, and use the expressions they want to hear. Treat everyone differently. Concentrate on your counterpart's specific situation, and analyse their inner and outer needs. Put yourself in their mind-set, and focus on their personality. Analyse their characters, strengths, and weaknesses. Understand what drives or hurts them. Create a connection, predict their emotions, and try to steer your argumentation accordingly. Use strong eye contact, and create an atmosphere of trust and cooperation.

Adjust your approach as soon as you encounter difficulties. Resistance is a sign of insufficient flexibility on your side. It does not matter what you say - what matters is what your counterpart understands. Never lose sight of your goal. Dominate through empathy instead of brute force. Earn respect by showing respect to others. Make people feel that their opinions are important. Let them think that their concerns are even more so your concerns. Hide your self-interest, stress actual similarities, and avoid negative messages as long as possible.

Charm fellow MEPs by acknowledging their status and highlighting their importance. Ask for their counsel, and show them your appreciation. Target their vanity, and allow them to feel superior. The more you make your colleagues like and admire themselves, the more you will boost their affection for you.

Show public servants your respect by sending them personal Christmas cards or inviting them for lunches. Comfort them in front of their colleagues by greeting them by their first names. Continuously express your gratitude for their hard work, and publicly honour their impressive expertise.

As a general rule focus proactively on achieving a personal bond with everyone you meet. Ask your employees to prepare for every scheduled meeting a short briefing on the expected guests and to scan their profiles for similarities with your personal background. Familiarize yourself with every detail in order to instantly connect with your targets. Schedule every meeting to last thirty minutes, but stay for forty-five. Give everyone you talk to the feeling that at that moment they are most important to you. Steadily gain everyone's sympathy, until they become accomplices to your goals. If sympathy is not enough, get their support through exchanging favours.

Exchange Favours

Exchanging favours is an integral part of the political game. By asking others for help, you can successfully gain their support. Swallow your pride, and confront fellow MEPs in person with any request you have. Appeal to their egos, and challenge them to prove to you that they can get things done. They will know that rejecting your request for a favour means risking losing your support. As long as they can expect to profit from you in return, they will avoid turning you down.

Once you receive a favour, delay its return as long as possible. When you are in their debt, it is in your targets' interest to maintain an alliance with you. The bigger the favour you ask for, the more your counterparts will hope to get in return, and the longer they will be inclined to support you. Use their opportunism for your own benefit.

Proactively grant favours to colleagues, who are facing difficult political times after a scandal or electoral defeat. MEPs getting support when they are on their knees tend to be more willing to form alliances.

In general try to accumulate what others want, and make them reliant on you. Focus on acquiring posts which give you access to scarce goods. Besides party and committee leadership positions, posts such as treasurer, coordinator, or queastor offer valuable possibilities in this regard. The more you can give or take away, the more support you will gain. Deal with anything you can. Help with appointments, share information, or trade media airtime. Keep track of who owes you what, and cash in when you can profit the most.

Always remember: money talks. The bigger your budget to spend, the bigger your network will be. Focus on maximising your resources by tapping into all possible revenue streams.

Do not do anything illegal. Keep your hands clean. Avoid everything that might endanger your or your employees' jobs. There is enough money to be distributed legally within the institutions. The budgetary committee finances hundreds of pilot projects all around Europe. The Parliament's bureau can decide to spend funds on almost any project related to European integration. Also your political group has unimaginable resources to work with. Study in detail all budgetary rules of procedure, and learn how to channel as much funds as possible to your electorate. Be persistent, and evermore ask for more.

Organise professional fund-raisers, and make sure

your website has an integrated fund-raising platform. Shield yourself from possible corruption attempts. Do not accept free meals and gifts. Do not profit financially from political favours. Any money you raise should always go directly to your party's treasurer. Provide transparency, and highlight how much money, and from whom, you have raised. At the same time, give donors the opportunity to share on your website their personal reasons for contributing.

Economize your resources. Almost every evening you see MEPs organising generous receptions providing tasteful canapés and champagne. Do not make the same mistake. Attend events rather than financing them. Do not waste your money on free drinks for your opponents' interns. Use your assets for expanding your network by making potential supporters dependent on you.

Focus in particular on gaining the domestic media's and your constituency's backing. Regularly buy advertisement spots in newspapers, and proactively fund events of your party at home. Take advantage of the institutional funds, and invite journalists and party leaders as your guests to Strasbourg and Brussels (see also sections 2.1 and 2.2). Introduce pilot projects that help domestic businesses, and organise patronages and grants for supportive local NGOs. The more favours you can provide to others, the more your influence will increase.

1.3

BUILD YOUR REPUTATION

The third key to gaining power is to earn the respect of your colleagues. Use it to create an aura of power nobody will dare challenge.

Impress others, and make a name for yourself. Do not just talk the talk but walk the walk. Work hard, claim your territory, and become known for being able to get things done. Build a reputation of power and success in order to get others to honour your standing. It is all about perceptions. Show that you are relevant. Prove that you matter. The more respect you can gain, the more influence you will have.

Concentrate on coming across as reliable and trustworthy. Stick to your commitments, and be loyal to your allies. Command the respect of opponents by being result-oriented and appearing unbiased. Cooperate constructively, and build bridges. The more trust you gain, the more influence you will have.

At the same time, create an image of strength by being resilient and unimpressed by resistance. Do not hesitate to question the authority of others. Passionately defend your principles, even against heavy opposition. The more you are known for being committed and persistent, the less people will want to fight with you.

Always keep up appearances. Avoid highlighting defeat or painful political concessions. Focus on coming across self-confident and sovereign. You are surrounded by alpha dogs waiting to grab your spot. Anticipate possible attacks, and confront anyone attempting to defy you. Take the initiative and transform your own shortcomings into strengths. Never let your guard down. Never show that you are stressed. Make it all look easy and natural. The more laid-back you seem when you achieve success, the more powerful you will be perceived as.

Gain respect without losing sympathy. Impress without being presumptuous. Remain credible and authentic. Lead without putting others down. The more professionally you handle your business, the more successful your colleagues will perceive you as.

Watch with whom you cooperate. Everything you do is a chance for self-advertisement. Portray yourself with well-known political leaders whose esteem and charisma can profit you. The more influential persons you are associated with, the more important you will be perceived as.

Do not combine forces with someone whose background you do not know. Check unknown MEPs' profiles and obscure think tanks' histories. Do not become a testimonial for anybody or anything you do not know. Always be careful. It takes a lifetime to build a reputation but only moments to destroy it.

Acquire Posts

Posts not only increase your ability to exchange favours but also are essential for gaining authority. The more posts you collect, the more important you will appear to voters and reporters.

Be alert after election. Groups and national delegations negotiate the distribution of posts, usually during the weeks before the legislature officially starts. There are hundreds of vacancies to be filled based on the D'Hondt method. Aim at obtaining as many titles as possible.

Put pressure on your national delegation and your group to involve you in the cross party negotiation process. Do not let anyone take a decision over your head. Never go away empty-handed. Be creative and look for additional title possibilities. If necessary, propose extra subcommittees and intergroups, or request temporary appointments and honorary roles. Do not compromise, until you can be chair or vice-chair somewhere.

Acquire further titles by becoming a member of respected NGOs and acting as a patron for esteemed events. Avoid taking up responsibilities that require a lot of work without offering any influence or prestige. The output always has to justify the input.

Demonstrate Competence

Knowledge is power. All information can one day be helpful. Therefore, use your posts for your advantage and gain access to internal studies, analyses, and polls. Trade essential information as a commodity to obtain additional information from others. The more you know, the more you will dominate.

Gain others' respect by creating an image of competence. No colleague, journalist, or lobbyist should ever catch you unprepared or uninformed. Work on your foreign language skills. Be always aware of the topics on the political agenda, and become an expert on each dossier you are responsible for. Demonstrate your knowledge continually, and show that you are involved. Publish exclusive briefing notes on controversial dossiers, and distribute consolidated versions of amended reports and opinions. Present yourself in the media as knowledgeable, and comment competently on every topic affecting your field of expertise. The more competent you are, the more you will be listened to.

Be Active

Every now and then, when calling the next speaker on their list, committee chairs mistakenly address a male MEP with *Ms* instead of *Mr.* What usually causes short laughter and a quick apology is in fact a disastrous public display of the lack of importance and limited impressiveness of the concerned MEP.

Avoid similar damage to your reputation by actively pursuing your career. Focus constantly on increasing your name recognition. The more politically active you are, the more known you will be, and the more important you will appear. Get involved and go to all committee, delegation, and group meetings. Attend conferences, be present in your constituency, and make sure you are regularly in the media. Avoid, however, juggling too many balls at once. Your presence should always maintain an aura of exclusivity. Stay focused on gaining respect, and do not go overboard with your initiatives. Being active should not become an end in itself.

At the same time, make sure your hard work is positively reflected in all public statistics measuring political activity. A low activity ranking based on objective parameters usually motivates reporters to question your worthiness of taxpayers' money. Concentrate constantly, therefore, on tweaking your numbers and maintaining a top position. A high ranking will gain you respect for being focused on the issues. It can outweigh a low media outreach and build your image as a dedicated and passionate politician.

Become responsible for regularly returning dossiers, table horizontal amendments on every accessible report and opinion, continuously table parliamentary questions and written declarations in reaction to current events, co-sign all supportable resolutions, and hand in written statements for every plenary debate. Make sure to rank higher than your fellow national delegation members, and use your lead to eliminate competitors when the list of candidates for the next election needs to be determined.

2

GET RENOMINATED

The goal of a successful MEP must always be reelection. The more terms you are in the EP, the more influence you will have and the more change you can achieve.

Most voters base their choices at European elections primarily on a party's national activities in the year before the election. It is therefore usually of limited relevance how successful you are in Brussels. Your election result depends mainly on your party's domestic actions.

What you can influence most in order to get reelected is your position on your party's list of candidates. The higher your party places you on the list, the more likely you will return to the Parliament. Consequently concentrate throughout your term on convincing your party leaders about the benefits your European work can bring to them and their electorate.

2.1

BE PRESENT IN YOUR CONSTITUENCY

The first key to be nominated again is to make everyone forget that you ever leave your constituency. Remain in the public awareness by staying actively involved in domestic matters.

MEPs are often surprised not to be renominated for another term after having achieved impressive legal reforms in their committees in the EP. They bitterly look down at the new nominees, whose only achievement in the past was to regularly attend insignificant get-togethers with local party members.

Do not end the same way. Never forget who can make or break you. Constituency work is the prerequisite of any lasting career in politics. If you would like to stay in the EP, you have to be present at home. The goal is not to win new voters but to gain the backing of the party. You need the local support to be nominated as a candidate, and you need the national support to achieve a promising position on the party's candidates' list.

Maintain an office and an apartment in your constituency to avoid being seen as an outsider. Regularly attend party gatherings, and accept meetings with local interest groups. Show interest in local developments, and pretend to be always within reach. Demonstrate your local roots by publicly displaying your affiliation with local sports teams and your respect for local traditions.

Stay involved in domestic politics by running for posts in the party. Try to obtain national and local leadership functions with influence on the party's strategic policy orientation. The more important titles you acquire, the more you can make your voice heard in public national debates. And even if you do not manage to obtain an influential national position, your candidature will increase your name recognition and demonstrate your readiness to take on additional responsibilities. As a consequence every opponent who got one of the powerful jobs you wanted will be motivated to keep you exiled from national politics and support your renomination for the EP.

Meet regularly with local and national journalists, and comment on domestic issues. Invite local reporters at the expense of the EP to Brussels and Strasbourg, and prove to them how hard you are working for your constituents. Show that you have not disappeared and are still keeping a tight watch on what matters most to your party and your voters. Focus on increasing your chances to be quoted in the domestic media by disseminating your European colleagues' press releases under your own name and including a national or local angle. Moreover, concentrate ceaselessly in your press work on demonstrating that you are important, competent and charismatic enough to win nationwide elections.

Build your image by continuously informing your party colleagues about your political activities. Ask your local party organisations to regularly post your press releases on their websites. In addition, produce regular newsletters and annual accountability reports and send them by e-mail to all party members. Make sure to highlight all your political work on the European, national, and local level and to list every media quote and public appearance. Even if most party members never read what you send them, they will remember that you are active and interested in staying in touch with them.

Build your support base within the party by attending as many local and national party congresses as possible. Always ask to be a speaker, and demonstrate your dedication to fight for the party's interests at home and in Europe. If you cannot attend, send pre-recorded video messages, and ask your local assistant to be your ambassador. Also support your party proactively in national and local election campaigns. Demonstrate throughout your term that, irrespective of your European duties, you will continue to find time to support your home base.

Stress your bonding with your local party by regularly organising local events and conferences. Get as many party members and constituents as possible to attend by choosing extraordinary venues and supplying free alcohol and food. Generate media attention by inviting impressive guests and debating polarising topics. Organise and pay for everything yourself, but share the spotlight with the party leaders. The aim is not to exchange information but to gain the respect and support of the local party members, who will decide about your renomination.

2.2

REPRESENT YOUR PARTY

The second key to be nominated again is to demonstrate your loyalty to your constituency. Convince constituents and party colleagues that you share their concerns and defend their interests.

Gain their support by giving them what they need.

In order to be put on the candidates' list, you have to prove throughout your term that you deserve to be renominated. Contact regularly, therefore, your local and national party leaders, and consult with them about how you could contribute to their domestic success. Show interest in their input, and promise to passionately fight for their objectives. Gain their confidence and build your reputation by convincing them that you can benefit them.

Your domestic party friends will not ask you what you have achieved for your country or Europe; they will want to know what you did for the party. Focus, therefore, throughout your term, on your party's interests, and subordinate your legislative and media work to the goal of upholding those party interests. Incorporate your party's objectives into your political initiatives, and as mentioned before, focus on channelling public funds to your party's electorate and supportive special-interest groups. Keep the leadership in the loop on controversial dossiers, and avoid attending roll-call votes where you would explicitly vote against the party line.

Take advantage of the fact that you can use the EP's phone for free, and ask your interns to regularly do polling and advertising for your political initiatives among local party organisations. Make use of the feedback you receive, and incorporate reasonable suggestions into your public communication. The more your party colleagues believe that you and they think alike, the more respect and support you will gain. If you cannot share the party's view on a given topic, communicate your disapproval in internal meetings. Never publically attack any party leader. As quickly as you may make it into the national press, no less quickly will you be removed from any promising position on the candidates' list. Disloyalty will always be punished. If you want to create an image of being independent and open-minded, address your public criticism to your European political group.

Regularly invite, at the expense of the EP, local and national party leaders to Brussels and Strasbourg and present yourself as their loyal representative. Assure them repeatedly of your gratitude for having obtained their confidence for representing them on the European level. Show them how hard you are working for them, and report on your progress in implementing the party's program. Demonstrate your importance by arranging meetings with influential European stakeholders. Gain your guests' sympathy by being humble and respectful and treating everyone like a state guest.

Make sure all party leaders return home with the impression that they can count on you.

Gain the party's gratitude by helping them to benefit the electorate. Buy promotional merchandise and produce practical leaflets about the direct benefits of your European work, and provide them to local party organisations. Allow them to add their logos to the merchandise, and motivate their leaders to contribute individual introductory notes to the leaflets.

Focus on creating an image of being close to the voters and being a dedicated representative of their interests. Always answer constituents' e-mails within twenty-four hours, and try to accommodate their requests in the best possible way. In addition, use your website as a tool to facilitate civic involvement, by enabling constituents to communicate their political concerns directly to you. Give them the chance to take part in online polls, to post their amendment proposals, or to chat with you live about controversial political topics.

Regardless of how little input you receive, use the public's feedback to justify your political initiatives and to create the impression that you speak not only for yourself or the party but also for the majority of the citizens. This will improve your standing in the party and enhance your bargaining powers towards political competitors.

2.3

SECURE A FRONT POSITION

The third key to be nominated again is to collect the party leadership's endorsement. Form alliances and outplay possible opponents to obtain a position on the candidates' list that will guarantee your return to the EP.

Focus throughout your term on gaining the majority's support for your renomination. The number of actual deciders in a party is usually limited. Make sure to identify the key players and to develop as early as possible targeted campaigns for gaining their individual endorsements. Build your support base step-by-step, and work your way up from local to regional to national leaders. Use every supporter you gain as an advocate towards your remaining targets.

Profile the relevant stakeholders by analysing their personal and professional backgrounds and aspirations. Find out whether they want money, influence, or respect. Investigate who their allies and enemies are and whose advice they are taking. Concentrate on detecting similarities and common objectives you can exploit to create a personal connection. Focus on satisfying their personal needs and benefitting their local party organisations. Gain their sympathies, and make it their own interest to prolong your career in the EP.

Analyse, on the European, national, and local level, the field of possible competitors for the leading positions on the candidates' list. Identify your strongest opponents, and calculate the size of their support bases. Consider how many of your opponents you would have to enter into coalitions with to represent jointly a voting majority within your party. Try to form an alliance with them in order to exclude all weaker contenders and to guarantee each member of the alliance a front position on the candidates' list.

If you do not expect to be able to form an alliance that will ensure your return to the EP, focus on eliminating the competition. Try to diminish your rivals' support base. Identify possible candidates who would appeal more to your competitors' supporters than to your own followers, and motivate them to run as well. Always play to win. Monitor every potential rival continuously, and identify possible points of attack. Keep track of their political activities and public statements, and record any shortcomings you find. Investigate rumours, pay attention to disloyal voting patterns, and search for disingenuous social media posts. Always retain enough incriminating material on your opponents to be able to shield yourself from their possible foul play.

3

STEER THE LEGISLATIVE PROCESS

Achieving change through steering the legislative process is the essence of all political work. The critical factor for being successful in it is ruthless pragmatism. Do not just hope for the success of your initiatives. Be strategic and brutally result-oriented in order to get them adopted. Be ready for conflict and able to compromise. Push your political agenda while focusing on securing necessary majorities. Fight passionately for your visions, but avoid wars you cannot win.

3.1

JOIN THE RIGHT COMMITTEES

The first key to steering the legislative process is to gain seats in relevant committees. Use your committee memberships to push your political agenda and benefit your political career.

Do not concentrate only on the committees which deal with issues you are personally interested in and have knowledge about. Choose committees which will improve your reputation, increase your influence, and boost your popularity.

Take into account your national media, your party, and your voters' interests to determine which committee might benefit you most. At the same time, study the statistics to analyse your political group's influence in the different parliamentary committees. Every political group is strong and influential in certain policy fields while being regularly outvoted in others.

The committees dealing with civil liberties, home affairs, the environment, public health, food safety, industrial policies, energy, the economy, monetary affairs, or international trade will allow you to work regularly on controversial and important dossiers. By being a member of one of the committees dealing with those issues, you can gain continuous media coverage and present yourself as an influential, passionate, and competent political heavyweight.

The committees dealing with consumer protection, internal market rules, legal affairs, transport, tourism, employment, or social affairs will gain the media's attention only from time to time. Your work, however, will have a direct and easily demonstrable impact on your voters' everyday lives. As a result, you will be able to portray yourself as a dedicated representative of the citizens' interests.

The committees dealing with regional development, the budget, agriculture, or fisheries are ideal for channelling public funds to your electorate. You may not get a lot of media coverage, but, by benefitting directly your party and your constituency, you can significantly increase your chances to be renominated.

Be careful about becoming a member of the committees dealing with foreign affairs, development, or constitutional affairs. These committees are very prestigious but have only limited powers. You might comment on issues in the press, but you will have very few opportunities to prove that you have actual political influence. In addition, it will be difficult to directly benefit your party or your voters through your legislative work.

All other committees usually have even fewer powers. Focus, therefore, as a member of those committees, on obtaining the reports that are most likely to create media coverage in your home country.

3.2

PICK THE BEST REPORTS

The second key to steering the legislative process is to become responsible for politically significant dossiers. Choose reports which will allow you to exert influence and improve your standing in the party.

Often eager MEPs fight to become responsible for files which are controversial and promise increased media coverage. These MEPs are blinded by their own egos and fail, therefore, to analyse the interests and powers of the other players involved. When years later the EP adopts their report with a fundamentally different content than the one they were fighting for, they have no other choice but to withdraw their names from their own reports.

Make sure you avoid similar harm to your reputation. Always position yourself strategically. In the European Parliament, there are neither permanent coalitions nor rigid government or opposition roles. As an MEP you can decide when to take responsibility. Depending on the issue, you can either be constructive and compromising or destructive and principled. Take a report only if you see a chance to successfully push your political agenda through. Be certain that you will be able to portray yourself as the political heavyweight who gets things done. When the majority in the EP want something your party and your voters are against, stay out of the game. Use your independence to assume responsibility only when you can profit from it.

Prepare your long-term strategies accordingly. Check in advance the Commission's legislative planning, and talk to lobbyists and supportive public servants in order to know when to expect which political initiative.

Analyse the political relevance of upcoming reports and how much media coverage they are most likely going to generate. Identify which MEPs will want to become responsible for these reports, and examine how controversial and time-consuming the negotiations consequently will be. Study the expectable national, political, and commercial interests that will be affected by the proposal. In addition evaluate how popular the practical implications of the expected reforms will be among your voters, your party, and the special-interest groups supporting your party.

Based on these deliberations, consider thoroughly which consequences a positive or negative outcome of the negotiations would have for your reputation and your long-term power aspirations. Identify your opportunity topics accordingly, and take all the subsequent necessary steps to become the responsible rapporteur on the concerned dossiers.

Your coordinator's support is essential in this regard. If he or she does not get you the reports you are interested in, your influence on the legislative work will be severely limited. Focus continually, therefore, on gaining your coordinator's sympathy and communicating as early as possible the files you want to be in charge of. Get your coordinator to confirm your responsibility before any competing group member is even aware that a legislative proposal is going to be presented.

If you do not get the reports you are interested in, make use of written declarations and plenary resolutions. Table them regularly on current topics, and sell them to the public as political initiatives you successfully managed to put on the European agenda. In addition, take advantage of the fact that many MEPs are reluctant to read the exact wording of every written declaration. Sneak in usually disputed political issues into otherwise harmless and generally acceptable texts, and use the MEPs' signatures to justify at a later stage concrete legislative amendments.

3.3

TABLE AMENDMENTS STRATEGICALLY

The third key to steering the legislative process is to prepare in advance an amendment strategy which will maximize your chances to get your initiatives adopted.

The more amendments you table, the more active you will seem. The more important and controversial your amendments are, the more media coverage you will gain. The more loyally your amendments represent your party's political line, the more party members and voters' respect you will gain. The more your amendments benefit the party and its electorate, the more likely you will be renominated.

Always remember: within the EP, it is easier to fight to keep a text unchanged than to fight to change it. Aim, therefore, at influencing legal proposals before their actual official presentation by the Commission. Try to obtain draft versions of the Commission's proposals, and communicate your concerns as early as possible to the heads of the responsible DGs as well as the relevant cabinet members of the involved Commissioners. Cooperate with your fellow group members, the press, supportive lobbyists, your permanent representation, and your Member State's and political family's Commissioners to increase the political pressure.

Once a legal proposal is officially presented, analyse thoroughly which parts of the file might cause controversy and which initiatives of yours might face resistance from other political or special-interest groups. Also, discuss your planned initiatives with selected journalists and lobbyists to get an advance sense of the public reactions your proposals will most likely receive. Prepare your political agenda accordingly.

If you are neither rapporteur nor shadow rapporteur, your impact on the file will be limited. The success of your proposals will depend mostly on the responsible rapporteur's and shadow rapporteurs' willingness to support your line. Therefore, limit your amendments' focus on your actually essential demands. Otherwise, the more amendments you table, the more chances the rapporteur and the shadows will have to pick and choose which of your demands they will want to support.

What is more, focus as much as possible on finding a wording for your amendments that the majority will most likely be able to support. Moreover, increase your proposals' political significance by motivating the rapporteur, the shadows, and as many influential allies from different political groups as possible to co-sign them.

Pretend from the start to be unbiased and cooperation-oriented in order to increase the other groups' readiness to consider your proposals open-mindedly. For this purpose always base a few of your amendments upon innocent proposals of opposing special-interest groups, and try to table them together with members of the other political groups.

Never forget: compromises are usually found in the political centre. If you cannot make it to the centre, make sure the centre finds you. Ask your colleagues to table enough extreme amendments to make the content and the amount of your demands look sensible and considerate.

Limit the possibility of legal and political arguments against your proposals by building the structure and logic of controversial amendments on existing precedents. Discuss your ideas as early as possible with the legal service, and ask them to provide you with previously adopted texts which had a similar content and wording. Furthermore, let lawyer linguists proofread your drafts before tabling your amendments.

In order to prepare for potential resistance towards your proposals, focus on producing as much external justification for your amendments as possible. As mentioned before, use the citizens' online feedback and your colleagues' response to your written declarations to justify your political agenda (see also sections 2.2 and 3.2).

In addition, produce further legitimation by creating the impression that your amendments are based upon impartial expert guidance. For this reason set up an informal expert group made up of lobbyists representing different conflicting interests, and take advantage of their contradictory feedback on how to amend the Commission's proposal. Table your amendments as you originally planned, but incorporate enough of their harmless suggestions to be able to present your proposals as an unbiased and fact-based reflection of the independent experts' recommendations.

Boost your initiatives' importance additionally by offering to table different Member States' proposals within Parliament in exchange for them tabling your amendments within Council. Cooperate with as many permanent representations as possible in order to increase your amendments' chances to make it through the Council and subsequently through the trilogues.

3.4
UNITE YOUR GROUP BEHIND YOU

The fourth key to steering the legislative process is to build a united power base behind your proposals.

The more united that outsiders perceive your group to be, the more influential it will be. Consequently try to make sure your fellow group members do not table too many contradicting amendments when you are responsible for representing these group members in the negotiations with the other groups. Approach your colleagues as early as possible with the aim of defining a common line you can all agree to follow.

Justify your proposals by presenting your colleagues with similar precedents which were previously adopted on the national level by members of your party family. Cooperate, therefore, in advance with local and national Members of Parliament in different Member States, and motivate them to incorporate your initiatives into their legislative proposals (or at least into their political resolutions at party congresses).

Unite your group behind your proposed line by making every colleague believe that you want the same thing that they do. In order to be able to convince them, make sure that your amendments position you politically in the centre of your group. As mentioned before, if necessary, get confidants in the group to table enough extreme proposals to make your initiatives look balanced. Once the deadline for amendments is over, mediate between the different opposing political camps within your group with the aim of maximising support for your proposals. Always present yourself internally as uniting and solution-oriented in order to be able to frame as dividing and fundamentalist those critics who are unwilling to agree with your line.

Take care of overeager colleagues who try to interfere in your negotiations with the other groups by suffocating these colleagues with your love. Instead of keeping secrets from them, overinform them. Overwhelm them with every material and e-mail you receive on the dossier, no matter how unimportant their content may be. Moreover, appeal to their egos by continuously asking them to provide you their opinions on new proposals. Keep them from working against you by making them work on the file.

Do not bother to disagree with permanently disruptive colleagues. While committee meetings are public, shadows' meetings are not. Hence, demand in committee what your colleagues want, and fight behind closed doors for what you want.

At the same time, curb your group's expectations by portraying the negotiations as tough and cumbersome. Prepare every group member to expect that difficult concessions will have to be made. The more the final compromise exceeds their expectations, the more ready they will be to support it.

Control precisely, therefore, the information your colleagues receive throughout the negotiations. Verify that the group's briefing notes are formulated concretely enough to motivate the majority to approve the presented file and at the same time vaguely enough to make sure your proposals do not attract enough attention to get rejected.

If despite all these efforts you are uncertain whether a majority in your group will actually be willing to back your proposals, prepare enough proxies for the group vote to be able to dictate your own fate.

3.5

NEGOTIATE WITH IMPACT

The fifth key to steering the legislative process is to negotiate with a ruthless focus on the desired end result.

Analyse the Terrain

Before determining your negotiation strategy, analyse in depth the interests and powers of all involved stakeholders. Never base your judgments on personal intuition alone. Profile thoroughly your negotiation partners in order to assess their strengths and weaknesses and in particular their trustworthiness. Identify their support bases among MEPs, journalists, and special-interest groups. Recognise who is influencing them. Find out what their personal, political, and national concerns are in order to understand the motivation behind their amendments.

Draw Up a Master Plan

Based on your analyses, draw up a plan containing all the steps you will take to make sure that there is no majority for an agreement you are not part of. Determine who you will combine forces with and on which issues. Assess what you will give up in exchange for which of their concessions. Consider how your rivals will try to push their agendas through and what countermeasures you will have to take. Evaluate which lobbyists and journalists you will use to play your opponents against one another. Focus always on the desired end results. Reflect throughout the negotiations on your existing chances for achieving your goals, and adjust your strategies if necessary.

Prepare Agreements in Advance

Do not wait until the first shadows' meeting to discuss possible deals. Avoid surprises by preparing private talks with every opponent you will need to cooperate with. Aim at pulling everyone to your side and finding bilateral agreements before the first round of official negotiations. Focus on establishing personal connections by convincing your opponents that their opinions and ideas matter to you. Do not lay all your cards out on the table. Adjust your arguments to the interests and concerns of every negotiation partner you meet with. Pretend to be sitting in the same boat. Get what you want by telling others what they want to hear. If necessary, share roles with your policy advisers in order to be able to communicate different messages to different targets.

Take the Lead

Once you have closed your bilateral deals, dominate the negotiations by taking the lead. Even if you are not the rapporteur, do not be shy of taking over the initiative. Be the first one to present and push for compromise amendments or negotiation lines for trilogues. Throw your opponents off guard. Be faster than everyone else is in order to make your proposals become the basis of the negotiations. Speed wins. Steer the debate by forcing your competitors to discuss along your lines.

Secure a Level Playing Field

Focus always on securing a level playing field. Compare your strengths and weaknesses with those of your opponents. Analyse everybody's rhetoric and negotiation skills as well as their expertise on the dossier and take all possible steps to even out your weaknesses.

If you lack supporters in the EP, organise e-mail and fax campaigns in support of your initiatives and send supportive lobbyists to work your opponents and their domestic party leaderships. In addition, motivate confidants to post supportive comments on social media sites or under online news articles regarding your issues, yourself, and your party.

If your foreign language skills are not perfect, push for your native language to be used during the negotiations, or use translators.

If you conclude that your opponents have more expertise on the dossier than you do, but you are confident that your advisers are more experienced than their advisers, request that technical meetings be held before every shadows' meeting. Let your employees prepare the ground for you, so that you have to focus only on closing the deals.

Control the Agenda

Influence the agenda with the aim of gaining an advantage over your opponents. Analyse your colleagues' usual flight times, identify the dates of their national holidays, and find out when their local and national elections are held. Exclude your opponents from the negotiations by scheduling meetings at times when they are less likely to be able to attend. Break news in the press when your competitors are on a delegation trip in an eight-hour different time zone and cannot react. Limit your rivals' chances to articulate their resistance to your proposals in front of a wider audience by putting your item on the committee's agenda at times when most MEPs are travelling back home to their constituents. Moreover, if it helps your interests, organise the voting at times when domestic elections force your opponents to be more careful and observant about the voters' expectations.

Bend the Rules to Your Favour

Never hesitate to abuse legal arguments to push through your political agenda. Take advantage of the legal service, and request it to verify the legality of every amendment you would like to see dismissed. In addition, exploit every rule of procedure which helps you enforce your interests. Refuse to vote if all the documents are not drawn up in all official languages. Refer to compulsory time limits in order to cancel unwanted debates. Furthermore, request that your confidants ask you blue-card questions, with the aim of prolonging your speaking time during plenary debates.

Eliminate Disturbers

Sideline every overambitious committee staff member who pushes your colleagues to defy your initiatives. Confront them aggressively and let them know that you are aware of their activities. If necessary, criticize them publicly in the committee meeting in order to force their hierarchies to take them off the file. Never believe in anybody's impartiality. Almost every public servant has a political agenda. Many have been working for a political group before. Even if they are bound to be neutral now, their convictions and networks have not disappeared.

Similarly, neutralize difficult parliamentary assistants if you realize that it is them and not their MEPs who are working against your proposals. Approach their MEPs when they are alone, and use the fact these MEPs are not too familiar with the file to pin them down to a deal that sounds reasonable but incorporates all your demands. If their assistants push them later to withdraw their consent to the deal, repeat the same procedure again, and suggest an alternative deal. The MEPs in question will usually be too embarrassed to take their word back twice.

Do Not Give In Too Early

Do not give in to bullying. Stamina is essential. Be ready to prolong the negotiations as long as necessary. Perseverance usually pays off. The longer you can maintain your demands without appearing unreasonable, the more you will win.

Compromise

Do not put too much pressure on your opponents, or they will turn emotional and therefore unpredictable. Ask for more than you need and then gradually give in on your demands in the course of the negotiations in order to make your opponents feel strong and successful. Portray yourself always as seeking compromise. Give in as much as necessary to gain the majority's support for your initiatives. Avoid going into full opposition. You always meet twice. Who is your enemy now, might be your partner on the next file. Do not burn bridges. Try to remain on speaking terms with your opponents even if you hate them. If you fight until you do not talk anymore, you will lose power. Isolation from your opponents cuts your access to direct information and limits your ability to exert influence. Avoid personal vendettas. Never fight for the sake of honour. Always try to deescalate conflicts and allow your opponents to save face.

Attack and Defeat

If war is inevitable, strike first. When your opponents are conspiring against you, be ready and able to go into conflicts.

If you are confronted with foul play, do not hesitate to attack and defeat your opponents. Stop looking for compromises, and start concentrating on your opponents' vulnerabilities. Challenge their authority in front of the other negotiation partners, and attack their personalities, their values, and their competences.

Eat or be eaten. Isolate and weaken your opponents by questioning their integrity and damaging their reputation. If necessary, suggest that they are leaking internal information to the press, or insinuate that they have a secret plan to let the negotiations fail. Create mistrust in order to destroy their support bases.

Combat immediately, transparently, and confidently any counterattack in order to restrict the public debate to your opponents' shortcomings. Moreover, ask confidants to attend your opponents' press conferences to make sure that the discussions evolve according to your expectations.

At the same time, attack your opponents repeatedly in their domestic media. Instead of highlighting all the points on which you disagree, stress mainly the ones on which your opponents represent a minority position. Portray your opponents as partisan and irresponsible. Increase the authenticity of your accusations by choosing arguments which reinforce existing stereotypes against your opponents and their political parties. Continually step up the pressure. Reduce your opponents to despair, and make them lose their confidence, until they are forced to retreat.

3.6

MAXIMISE YOUR VOTES

The sixth key to steering the legislative process is to secure a stable majority in favour of your political initiatives. Verify in advance the necessary head count, and make sure that everyone who promises to support you actually attends the votes.

Never put a minus on a voting list if you do not have to. Accept that some MEPs table stupid or senseless amendments. As long as these amendments do not contradict your political goals, leave it to the Member States to eliminate them during trilogues. Do not make enemies for the sake of being right. Focus, rather, on maximising your support base.

Never leave votes to chance. Avoid surprises by continually calculating expectable majorities. If necessary, go fishing for votes among MEPs within opposing political groups. Lobby passionately for your amendments, and try to break up political alliances by appealing to MEPs' diverging national interests. Make deals and exchange favours. Be aware for which reasons which MEPs and national delegations usually deviate from their political group's line and use the information to pull them over to your side. In addition, identify undecided non-attached MEPs, and gain their support by offering them future cooperation opportunities on common parliamentary resolutions and written declarations.

If you cannot avoid being outvoted, focus on intensifying your cooperation with the Member States, which supported your amendments within Council, and work them to push your proposals during trilogues.

3.7

CONTROL THE TRILOGUES

The seventh key to steering the legislative process is to remain unyielding to the pressure of the other institutions. Stand your ground, and do not concede without profiting.

Many MEPs make the mistake of relying fully on the rapporteur to represent their interests during trilogues. At the same time, many rapporteurs make the mistake of relying fully on the Council presidency to represent the interests of all twenty-eight Member States.

Be wiser. Do not rely on anyone but yourself. All institutions, political groups, and Member States will aim at securing their own interests first, before representing anyone else's. There is no selflessness in politics. Stay actively involved in the trilogue negotiations, and maintain close ties to all relevant stakeholders to ensure that no Member State or political group makes deals over your head.

Establish close ties with different permanent representations to be able to find out at any time what is going on within Council. Identify the Member States that have an interest in your dossier, and recognise in which coalitions they are fighting for and for which issues. The more stakeholders you cooperate with, the better you will know whose interests to play against another's.

Take the lead, and influence the Member States through all possible channels, with the aim of gaining the support of a qualified majority within Council. Find allies among Member States, and work together to steer the debate in parallel in both institutions. What is more, ask supportive MEPs whose parties are in government on the national level to get their Ministers to push your agenda within Council.

While working the Council, do not forget to keep the EP united behind your initiatives. Pretend continuously that your amendments are receiving strong support among Member States, in order to maintain the Parliament's backing for your proposals. Keep close ties to all your amendments' co-signatories from the other groups, and motivate them to push their shadows to remain firmly behind your political agenda. Safeguard your own group's solidarity by reassuring every group member that their interests are loyally defended throughout the negotiations.

At the same time, do not underestimate the significance of the Commission's influence during the negotiations. Every DG has its own political interests and will use all its manpower, strategic experience, and expertise to defend them.

Be always aware that both the Commission and the Council are bound by their predetermined negotiation mandates. Most public servants are creative and compromise-oriented but forbidden to take political decisions without prior authorisation. Ministers and Commissioners are usually more open to political deals. They have a personal interest in quick results and are more focused on the public perception of an agreement. Consequently, if you hit a dead end with the public servants, be ready to escalate the negotiations until the responsible Minister and Commissioner are forced to take over.

Escalate the talks by withdrawing prior concessions and increasing your demands. Instead of giving in to any of the other institutions' requests, offer to incorporate their concerns into recitals and nonbinding declarations. Show that you know how to play their game. Do not get intimidated by their uncompromising proposals. Summon, rather, the responsible Minister and Commissioner to appear in front of the committee to justify publicly their ignorance towards the EP's democratically determined political concerns.

Do not hesitate to use the press to exert constant public pressure on every negotiation partner. If necessary, show your determination by threatening to freeze selected budget lines that are of imminent importance for the other institutions. At the same time, work the Parliament's Conference of Presidents to postpone agreements on other files, until an agreement on your file is achieved.

Keep the pressure up and demonstrate your power ruthlessly, until the talks are lifted from the technical to the political level and the other institutions are finally ready to make deals that meet the Parliament's demands halfway.

4

GAIN PUBLIC SUPPORT

Support among voters and media representatives is a prerequisite for political success. The more public support you and your initiatives have, the more readily your group will follow your lead, and the more reluctantly your opponents will dare vote down your amendments. At the same time, the more known and appealing to the general public you are, the more likely your party will be willing to renominate you. Focus, therefore, throughout your term on gaining regular positive media exposure and positioning yourself publicly where the party and the voters want you to be.

4.1

APPEAL TO YOUR TARGET AUDIENCES

The first key to gaining public support is to appeal

to the public's needs.

Instead of trying to appeal to all citizens, focus first on the audiences which are most likely to support you. Study for this reason the last decade's European, national, and local election analyses, and examine the demographics of your party's electorate. Distinguish the age group, gender, education, occupations, and locations your party most appeals to. In addition, recognise the issues and competences of your party which attract most public support.

Consequently, gain your target audiences' trust and support by aiming your media work at their preferences and priorities. You are your product. Appeal to your targets' minds and hearts. Focus on creating an authentic brand and message, which differentiate you from your competitors and demonstrate to your target audiences that you stand for what they desire.

Promote your strengths and assets, and present yourself as a charismatic, competent, and trustworthy leader. Represent your targets' interests, and communicate the benefits you strive to achieve for them. Build your brand by staying consistently on message and making sure that your actions, demeanour, and appearance correlate with it.

Get Your Messages Across

Media in the twenty-first century is headline-centred. Repackage your messages into short, simple, and quote-worthy statements. Break the big picture down to attention-grabbing examples and memorable stories. Avoid abstract and complicated facts. Use plain language and an authentic conversational tone. The goal is to get understood, not to educate. Always bear in mind your audience's knowledge.

Never forget: media needs emotional, black-and-white arguments. Present competing legal initiatives, therefore, always as emotional and controversial conflicts about diverging political principles. Define a problem, name the guilty, and present the solution. Try to create fear and hope at the same time. Be eloquent and provocative, and use forceful expressions. Stand out and dare to be original. The more good quotes you provide the media, the more often they will return to ask for more.

Decide before every public statement and speech how you want to position yourself. Determine in advance the audience you want to target, how you want to be perceived, and which message you want to deliver. Prepare your statements and speeches accordingly. The goal of a public statement or speech is not to present facts but to connect with and win over your target audience. Irrespective of your actual plans, do not talk about what you want but about your audience's concerns and how your actions will profit their lives.

Interviews are just another opportunity to get your message across. Always focus first, therefore, on the message you want to deliver, and second on the response to the question you are supposed to answer. Charm your interviewer, but communicate to your target audience. Do not hesitate to take your time to think about your answers. It is your responsibility to make sure that nothing you say can be taken out of context. In general avoid being spontaneous. Always rehearse before interviews. Formulate in advance authentic and clear-cut answers to every possible question, and prepare the punchy quotes you want to see published.

4.2

GAIN PUBLICITY

The second key to gaining public support is to get continuous publicity.

Many MEPs make the mistake of limiting their media work's focus to their committees and reports. Be more outgoing. The content of your media and legislative work do not have to overlap. The more publicity you gain, the more chances you will have to get your messages across in order to attract new voters and to exert pressure on your opponents. Monitor the national and international media, and jump on every bit of breaking news that is remotely connected to your political work and is relevant to your constituents. The more quickly and originally you react to breaking stories, the more likely you will run in the media.

Regularly lay down short- and long-term media action plans. Most major stories are foreseeable. Maintain your public presence by proactively managing the news. For this reason analyse the work programs of all local, national, and European institutions and bodies. Moreover, study the drafts of every forthcoming announcement, declaration, and proposal. Focus on identifying controversial and newsworthy matters in advance. Be prepared and ready before everyone else is in order to become the competent contact person for the media. Formulate press releases, op-eds, and social media postings in time to publish them before or simultaneously with the breaking story.

Beyond reacting to ongoing events, try to generate news yourself. Always remember: to be able to sell, you need to have a winning product. Focus continually, therefore, on creating content which is of value for the media. Leak confidential proposals, expose scandals, or just add a spin to ongoing matters by tabling issue-related parliamentary questions, written declarations, and resolutions. The more exclusive and significant information you can provide, the more publicity you will gain.

Concentrate during the parliamentary recess on reputation-building media activities. Visit victims of a natural disaster, plant closing, or crime, and take the national press with you. Do internships at local businesses and NGOs, and invite the local press to join you. Organise charity events, and co-operate with the boulevard media on promoting them. Take part in awareness-raising campaigns, and advertise them on your social media sites. Focus constantly on building your name recognition without blurring your political profile.

Exploit Every Media Channel

Always remember: if you are out of sight, you are out of mind. Thus, maximise your public outreach by focusing on the entire media spectrum. Use television, radio, wires, magazines, newspapers, blogs, video platforms, Internet portals, and social media for delivering your messages. Create as many synergies as possible by repackaging the same message over and over, but make sure to adjust your approach to the specific tool you are using, including the following:

Press Releases

Issue a press release only if you have something to say and there is a news moment for it. Create a database of local, national, and European media contacts, and distribute your press releases to them according to their field of competence and their media's target audiences. Increase your chances to get quoted by asking your office to personally pitch your strongest statements to the responsible reporters, editors, and producers. Meet the media's deadlines early enough to not only get your quotes published but also to influence the actual perspective of the story.

Social Media

Social media offer the most direct and independent way to deliver your messages. While social networks appeal to a mass audience, microblogs usually appeal to more specific audiences, such as news media representatives, politicians, party members, activists, and special-interest groups. Use your tools accordingly. Microblogs offer the fastest way to publish a newsworthy quote regarding breaking news. A social network page offers the best opportunity to maximize your outreach and build your audience.

The more actively you use social media, the more people will follow your messages. Concentrate, therefore, on posting up-to-date, engaging, and provocative content, and make sure to react to the feedback you receive. Entertain your followers while delivering your political messages. Keep your posts to one or two sentences, use plain language, be direct, take sides, and include a picture. Make sure to invest in targeted advertising to build your audience and increase your followers' engagement. The more your content gets shared, the more followers you will gain and the more important your party will perceive you as.

Personal Website

Make your website your general hub to provide in-depth information about yourself and your activities. Publish all your press releases, media coverage, social media posts, videos, and pictures. Highlight your main political achievements, and demonstrate your local roots. What is more, use your website as a platform for fund-raising and civic involvement (see also sections 1.2 and 2.2).

Online Encyclopaedias

Online encyclopaedias are the first source for most people to find objective information about you and your political work. Consequently use online encyclopaedias to build your reputation, and make sure that they extensively highlight your strengths and successes.

Television

The best way to get into popular national TV shows is to be impressive on local TV first. Lure the producers and the audience through offering unique perspectives and provocative statements. For news interviews boil your messages down to ten-second sound bites. Always remember: on TV your appearance is at least as important as the substance of your message. Therefore always practice your performance in advance to make sure that your tone, facial expressions, and body language reinforce your confidence and message.

Cooperate with Media Representatives

The more you cooperate with the media, the more publicity you will gain. The better your relationship with news media representatives is, the more likely your viewpoint will be mirrored and incorporated in their publications.

Identify, therefore, the reporters, bloggers, editors, producers, and publishers who are covering the topics you are working on, and concentrate on sparking their interest in you. Demonstrate that you are not only competent and entertaining but also able to provide a unique perspective to their audiences.

If your profile fails to attract enough attention among reporters, try to seduce them. Pay their lunches to get them to meet with you. Offer them secret documents and internal rumours in exchange for positive coverage. Do their jobs by providing them with ready-made, accurately documented scoops. What is more, appeal to their needs by repeatedly tabling written declarations and resolutions demanding more media subsidies and respect for press freedom.

No matter how good your relationship with media representatives is, never let your guard down. No reporter will ever hesitate to destroy you in order to get a cover story. You need them more than they need you, and they know it.

EPILOGUE

Political success is a conscious decision. Master the arts of gaining influence and popularity, and take the lead by setting your goals high.

Do not be satisfied until you dominate the entire political landscape. You are ready. Overshadow the competition, and become the undisputed front runner for the next election. Put your beliefs into action, and do what is necessary.

Never settle. Dare to make a difference. Dare to make history.

MARILYN POLITICAL

Marilyn Political is a consulting company advising political leaders. Its core business is to make political careers excel. It supports its clients in steering the legislative process, gaining publicity, and securing their reelection. It delivers best practice, battle-tested advice, combined with result-oriented execution.

---

www.marilynpolitical.com

Made in the USA
Charleston, SC
15 January 2017